Wildflowers Plucked
From The Concrete Jungle

GW00470421

Jeanette Santos- Strong

BookLeaf
Publishing

Wildflowers Plucked From The Concrete
Jungle © 2022 Jeanette Santos- Strong

Presentation by *BookLeaf Publishing*

Web: www.bookleafpub.com

E-mail: info@bookleafpub.com

ISBN: 9789357615372

First edition 2022

This book is dedicated to my husband Mr. Strong for loving, believing and investing in me since day one, and holding my hand through the waves of this writing journey.

Our children, Peewee, Zaya, Tatt, Nova, Cande, Gordo, Diamond, Lala, and Selwyn for being my rocks and reasons and why I push so hard for a better tomorrow. (Love you guys so much!)

My siblings Jenn, Jess, Jai, and Jas for staying strong and beautiful no matter what life handed them. (It wasn't easy but we made it)

My mom and dad for trying their best. May they continue to Rest In Peace.

My Abuela, for her sacrifices, unconditional love and hard lessons.

My aunts Mari, and Titi who helped raise me and always showed me unconditional love.

My cousins, you guys rock! Forever!

My Bestie Gee, for the amazing ten years of friendship, and for always being my top fan.

My extended family, and friends who contributed to supporting me throughout my life and made a positive impact in it.

ACKNOWLEDGEMENT

First and foremost, I would love to take this time out to thank my creator, the most high for never failing me, always guiding me, blessing me with perseverance, and giving me the talent of imagination and writing.

Thank you to my supporters who relate, and believing in my work.

Thank you to my readers, may you take away an empathetic experience from the words of my heart.

A huge Thanks to all my fellow SA and DV survivors for being courageous. None of us are ever alone.

Last but not least, to BookLeaf Publishing for this opportunity.

PREFACE

In this book you will encounter a collective of poems that stemmed from my old diaries, and life experiences I've jot down throughout my years, some are old some are new.

Many were the times when my brain turned into mush trying to recollect my feelings towards certain situations for this project.

When you've had a rough childhood, and you've survived abuse, speaking about it is soothing, but writing about it is cathartic.

We lived in a world where speaking and writing about your feeling was looked down upon. Simply because family members were embarrassed, or afraid of the truth.

It took bravery to put this collection together.
Some will love it,
some will dismiss it.

This book is intended to reach those who can relate and those who may care to support me. Enjoy!

169 & Prospect

169 and Prospect Ave.
Where her dreams took life,
then shortly turned to ash.

Home sweet home of a young
girl's nest,
Striped out from her skin,
the start of her bitterness.

With cookies, and candies they bribed.
All that burst of goodness a child shouldn't
deny,
but tricks and hicks of the wicked minds
consumed her,
dimming her light.
The beginning of all her prescribes.

Left in the presence of evil,
Some loved to touch, others loved to watch.
Another innocent victim on someone's
notch.

What was supposed to remain innocent as
long as innocent could,
was quickly tainted.
The sickened minds controlled her fears,
Forced actions flooded her eyes with tears.

Not knowing right from wrong,
she juggled through the hands of preys.
The figure of her flower now in dismay.
Thought and emotions grew unsure,
But she still embraced she had pure.

169 and Prospect Ave.

Sometimes

I look around for that voice I can't hear,
I search and I search… into my mind,
I probe into the deep thoughts of my brain.
But that is the spot I can't approach without
fear,
Sometimes.

I hunt for answers that I don't believe,
I chase and I chase… into my emotions,
I scavenge the deep chambers of my heart.
But that is the area that I can't address
without grief,
Sometimes.

I dig for that intuition I can't ingest,
I forage and I forage… into my spirit,
I quest the deep wilderness of my soul.
But that is the realm that I can't sustain
without distress,
Sometimes.

I quit searching, I quit probing,
I quit hunting, I quit chasing,
I quit scavenging, I quit foraging,
and I quit questing for me.
I'm letting sometimes turn to seldom, and
seldom into never…
Sometimes.

Little Brown Flowers in the Midst

There they were, lost in the Midst.
Beautiful flowers sowed in concrete,
Ejected by the habits of their father's sins.
Childhood memories are bittersweet.
With a thousand words they describe my skin,
But the silence of their words cry from overruled sins.
My little Brown Flowers in the Midst.

There they were, alone in the Midst.
Bright stars radiated in vast obscurity.
Consumed by the lust of their mother's secrets.
Nurtured to benefit society's itch,
Snatched from security, it's far from a glitch.
My little Brown Flowers in the Midst.

There they were, afraid in the midst.
Warriors on the battlefield of fate.
A million acts today are shown to describe
the hate.
Frightened by the minds of beasts who feed
on them,
Inheriting the dusts of yesterday's condemn.
My little Brown Flowers in the Midst.

There they were, segregated in the midst.
Goddess' ruling in false kingdoms,
Revealing reigns against royal venoms.
Conditioned by ratified illusions.
Awakening to new dawns of rest,
Swaddled in faded cultivated crests.
My Little Brown Flowers in the Midst.

There they are, standing in the Midst.
Rebuilding birth, and preserving un-winged
souls,
Trailblazers fighting against the forced roles.
From ameliorating shields, to protecting
fields.
Regenerating roots to heal tomorrow's past,
While rejoicing to the creators vast.
My Little Brown Flowers in the Midst.

There they sow, rooted in the Midst.
Reaping the harvest of tomorrow's fall,
While Quintessential to their call.
Forever guarding the wild's chanting,
Promised visions inheriting our
Matriarchy's marching...
Brown Flowers in the Midst.

When I found Home

It wasn't when I entered this world because I
didn't ask to be here. I didn't design the
paths of this place, let alone chose it.
It wasn't the sugar-coated moments of
happiness my parents gave us to eat after
every boxing match.
It wasn't the moment when I was snatched
from my mother's arms at the age of seven.
The warm summer breeze of that night gave
me a glimpse of people's destructive
obsessions.
It wasn't the fear I felt every time I walked
through the doors of five different foster
homes. The idea of a loving family faded,
and frantically I've grown.
It wasn't the comfort of the ones who tried to
raise me, nor the uniformed trust from all
the therapists who wanted to fix me. I
couldn't find coziness in their efforts
because, in most cases, it was only their job.
It wasn't all the places I ran to for help;
every time I needed to dodge a black eye,

because the black eyes turned into false
narratives of love, over and over and over.
It wasn't the best houses I tried to provide
my children, nor buying them all the things
they wanted. Because the most valuable
possessions I provided my children with are
not material at all.
The journey home began when I took a
glimpse into her soul.
My mother's soul was immensely scorned,
but she disguised herself as the life of the
party wearing armor.
As she expressed to me that she wanted to
raise me, but couldn't; the tears flooded her
eyes. Then, I knew what her "couldn't"
meant.
Her eyes explained it all, every day.
I found the meaning of a place called home
through my mother's eyes. Yet, as they told
her story, they also felt her pain and joy.
I found the meaning of a place called home
when I empathized with my mother,
enduring her failures and strengths.
Only then, did I find forgiveness.
Only then, I realized when I found Home.

Not Today!

Today I realized that I have to let my demons go. Even though they comfort me they can't stay.

The many times they took me in, it felt good. But, that's the very thing that makes them no good for me.

Time to clean every inch of my mind, body and soul of the hauntings that keep me trapped in the house of my horrors past.

It's time to put them down as much as they let me put myself down.

Time to crucify them as much as they crucified my dignity, the light of who I was meant to be.

As I sit here in my living room taking off my jewelry, I rumble with myself. Half of me is joyfully returning to the once modestly fierce woman she truly was.

The other half is slaying her demons one by one, while they invisibly pull her soul down to the dark side.

The roots of my mother's land is slowly withering, the nourishment of its fruits nourishes no more.
So as I sit here taking off the last bracelet, I lean back with dignity.

The last demon clings to life grabbing on to my ankle.
I took a deep breath, and elevated my foot stumping with crap out of it.

Not today!, ghost of ego, no more.

Toxic Love

I didn't realize I was trapped in a toxic love
'cause I was too busy day dreaming on the
ideas of what it could be, rather than what is
truly was.

The kind of love that took my integrity
away, just to feed the ego of the beast I sleep
with every night.

The kind of love that took my breath away,
but then knocked wind out my chest.

The kind of love that made me feel loved
while playing a fool to not look like a fool.

The kind of love that preyed on my
goodness, tainting my train of thoughts from
pure sanity.

I realized late, but better late than never. I
conquered toxic love.
The windows of my heart opened up wide,
and I snapped out the dream of this idea that
wasn't mine.

A toxic love slowly left to die.

When He Makes Me Crawl
Out of My Dark

When he makes me crawl out my dark,
It happens so fast, that sometimes
I don't even notice is past.

It was like,
Walking in the middle of the forrest,
In the vast of morning,
The sky was sexy as dark,
Illuminated by the eternal moon, so sacred,
so soft.

The only sounds I heard was the silent
nostalgic cries
of the creatures, but every step a cracking
branch.

My body quivered with every feel of his
cool touch.
Suddenly, his prowling eyes pulled me,
And they lit up when he kiss it.

Every second of fusion,
my flesh embedded with the earth.

The faster his breath sung, the deeper he
savaged.
Then came the healing of his ravage.

And as the morning grew warmer,
The creatures scattered into the horizons.

I opened my eyes to the sun gleaming,
The wind blowing on my face so gentle, so
warm.

And the sound of my day,
was the song of the creatures play,
When he makes me crawl out my dark.

Like Candy

I was told that it would taste like Candy.

I was told that the first time would be like a
burst
Of sweetness on your tongue that will
forever linger.

Well, I don't know if it was that my taste
buds weren't savoring flavors those nights,
Or if I just got the wrong kind of candy.

Was it bitter chocolate?
Or the a sweet and sour
 fruity delight?
Was it sweet, then sour?
Or Sour from the first taste?

Hershey's, Snickers, Jolly Ranchers,
And Swedish fish…
Lollipops, Jaw breakers, Cupcakes,
Oreos, and Whatchamacallits too.

I kept searching for that sweet to my taste,
I kept trying to taste and taste, taste.

I've had my share candy after candy.

But it wasn't the taste of candy that my soul
was longer for,

it was a sweet touch.

I Didn't Sign Up For This

I Didn't Sign up for this,
not for judgement that hangs over the hills
of society,
making me feel inadequate because I don't
dress a certain way.

Not for Racism that is freely occupying
places,
that doesn't have room for it.

Not for blame constantly put on those who
are trying
to overcome burdens, from those who blame
them.

Not for the Control smoothly forced up on
our kids
via social media, trends and idols,
leading them further away.

Not for the Fear of statistics put in our
hearts,
making me feel less than the environment I
live in.

Not for the pressures placed by celebrities,
music videos, billboards or vogue
magazines.

Making me feel like I'm not woman enough
if I didn't have big boobs,
big ass and little waist.

I didn't sign up for this,
I just want to live judgment, racism, blame,
control, and pressure free.

100 Miles Within My Heart

100 miles of sadness that filled up the walls
of my ventricles leaving them drained and
dark.

100 miles of agony that clustered my
chambers leaving no room for air.

100 miles of joy that lit up the runways of
my aorta, leaving them enlightened for sure.

100 miles of fear that froze my valves,
Leaving them paralyzed and vague.

100 miles of shame that flooded the gates of
my arteries,
Leaving them drowned and hidden.

100 miles of excitement that fluttered
through my atriums, leaving them filled of
endless pleasure.

100 miles of anger that spread viciously
through my chambers, leaving them bitter
and betrayed.

100 miles within my heart that you never
knew.

Arson War

I dove into the core of his desires.

Appraising every
Fantasy,

Arousing every vessel,
I activated every alarm.

Burning up in flames,
Beginning of Arson war.

Younger Me

You were young and frail,
barley making it through the days.

The ignorance you carried,
was the shield of your pain.

You were reckless and free,
Always rebelling from what makes you
afraid.

The innocence you held on to,
Was the purest of it's remains.

You were intelligent and meek,
usually seeking knowledge, and
strengthening the weak.

Your emotions were a mess,
but your mind wasn't something you contest.

You were a visionary and a dreamer,
always putting pen to paper.

Your endurance and your strive,
we're the writings of your strife.

Younger me,
you give me life.

This Morning Was A Little Different

This morning was a little different,
It wasn't as sunny as when the sun kisses
my crown at sunrise.

The air was a little chilled, and the remnants
of the fog still lingered through the rays.

The plan for today was to soar a little higher
than yesterday's skies.

To get up from bed and give it another try.

I gazed out my window, the condensation
was heavy on the sill.
It was another day to seek a thrill.

This afternoon was a little skeptic.
It wasn't as occupied as most days when my
mind has lots to do.

The agenda for today was to seek a little
deeper than yesterday's
surface and to give it another go at my
purpose.

I walked out my door, the traffic had a
different rhythm.
It wasn't flowing as usual, it lacked
algorithm.

I gave it a rest, changing plans was the best.

I put on my pajamas, and dove into the stare
of the night.

Hopefully, tomorrow's morning feels a little
different.
Hopefully, the sun kisses my crown at
sunrise.

Belonging

A little girl looking for the place they call
home,

That she can also call her own.

Every few months to a year, I traveled
within the system.

I often saw my life in bags, favorite spot, by
the door.

A new borrowed home, I couldn't call it my
own.

Every bedroom was dressed to impress.

My reality began to haze, once the tidal
waves of all the different

cultures, habits, parenting skills,

and rules cluttered my brain.

Things I was allowed to do in one foster home,

wasn't allowed in the other.

From the clothing to the food,

everything changes, even the moods.

After the third home, I didn't see myself anymore.

Confusion set it from the pressures of having to

learn new families, new rules and new schools.

It was hard keeping up with all those identities.

There were more first days of school, then lasts.

All over again, new teachers, new friends and new bullies.

Like a traveling gypsy I became immune to

dodging the roots.

Meanwhile the system lacked stability,

And it trickled down to my security.

Many versions of myself were developed in
the system.

Pieces of me were left in some foster homes,

And there were foster homes that left pieces
in me.

Society also played a part, in tearing me
apart,

All the stigmas and the lies they stamp on a
foster child,

It sometimes left my mental in disbelief.

Many times it was tiring,

even as a child the world can stress.

All I had were illusions, of a permanent address.

A little girl looking for the place they call home,

That she can also call her own.

Intuitions

I've felt like my intuitions failed me,

but after further evaluation,

I've failed my intuitions.

My Father

My father was a man, and the son of a man.
A man who tilt his earth, land nourished his
land.
A country Caribbean soul, who loved his
straw hats and loved ridding his tricycle
barefooted down the dirt roads.

Six foot 1, he took a stand, that wasn't even
counting the inches of his curly afro.
He wasn't a saint and he doubled as a sinner,
but I remember many times he cooked us
delicious dinners.

He knew forgiveness, and had wisdom,
Also practiced love, he was patient.

He knew laughter and he knew pain.
His stern lessons, had much to gain.

A wild hibiscus, stole his heart.
It was love at his sight.

A crown on his head but yet a thorn on
both sides as created he life, after life,
after life.

My father was a man, and the son of a man.

Today, tomorrow and always he'll always be
my father.

B-Cups

Every time I shopped at Victoria's Secret,
I got intimidated by the the soiree of women
Parading their large protruding cleavages in
face.

I'd pick up a bra,
admire the lace and the style,
"Ooh, I'm about to see if they have this my
size"

But then, I'd put it right back.
I knew it wouldn't fit me like it would
the women in front of me.

My insecurities about my B-Cups
began in middle school.

At the age a teen starts to develop
in ways unimaginable ways.

In route to my next class, walking down the
halls,
the boys in my class would call my name,
And slap the wall.

It was mandatory to wear padded bras all the
time.
It boosted my self esteem, that isn't a crime.

Sometimes I'd even stuff my bras,
To give me a boost with the new boy in
class.

They've held on tight and gone through
changes,
But my B cups were never mistaken.

My confidence began to flourish
around my late twenties.

Three kids later and still they remained
perky.

Through thick and thin they've
They're part of my personality, quirky.

Through thick and thin they never failed me.
Not even a complaint,

I walked into Victoria's Secret,
Only this time, I didn't get intimidated
by double dd's or even c's

I beautifully laced hot pink bra,
To dress up my B-Cups.

Too much of a mouth full
is a waste anyway.

I Covered Up My Bruises to Love You

I put on a little extra concealer on my eyes
last week.
I wasn't in the mood to answer questions.

I hid the pain, I had to be strong
My babies needed mom it pretend there was
nothing wrong.

The knuckles on your fists, engraved with
my name.
I know they hurt too, they're just used to the
pain.

I covered up my bruises to love you.

A little more foundation around my neck.
The imprints of your hands decorated my
skin.
I just had to take a deep breath.

Every other day, I switch out my makeup,
Wondering what part I had to cover today.

A little more blush on my cheeks,
I forgot a scuff mark.

I covered up my bruises to love you.

The tone of your voice paralyzed my
thoughts,
I'm ready today, to take the fault.

The darkness of your eyes told me you were
sick,
But every time you feel this way, I get
kicked.

A few days ago, I bandaged up my leg,
The imprinted tires left my side to beg.

A little more seclusion, my family in
disarray.

I covered up my bruises to love you

The make-up ran out, and I'm not buying
anymore.

My flesh is deteriorating, my spirit is sore,
and I know you're tired of this war.

Another day I wanted to live, to feed my
kids again.
My wounds had to heal, if not right now,
then when.
I covered up my bruises to love you.

Nemesis Poem

Drag yourself through the path of my feet,
Drink from the poison I consumed in my
heat.

Dive into the despair of my veins.
Have a taste of this flame.

If in my eyes you wish to stare,
It'll be my treat to watch you dare.

Free-fall into the desires of your heart,
Never say I didn't warn you, when it tears
you apart.

Rhythm Of My Story

Only chaos, peace, strong and the weak are
the forces
that collide through this heaven and hell.

My experiences, choices and my attitude are
the elements that reflects
through my life and death.

Opportunities to seek, hide, find, and expose
the in between, the above, the underneath.

Through it, in it and out, the side lines
sitting tragedy and doubt.

The ghosts of my past determined to haunt
me,
The Spirit of my future motivates me.

Words are sometimes forgotten, but scars
remain.
A phrase too familiar to my pain.

Negative spaces of differences will
diminish.

In the fire, or out in the cold,
The rhythm of my story never gets old.

Wildflowers Plucked From the Concrete Jungle

We were the definition of young and free.
Making memories in the streets of NYC.

Our summers were a blast
 we snuck out to pools, walked the FDR,
Even hung out by 116 & Park

We took advantage, broke some rules,
And all the stupid things teenagers do.

Corners of this voluptuous city
has the traces of our faces,

We were wildflowers plucked
 from the concrete jungle.

We were the definition of young and free.
Making memories in the streets of NYC

From Spanish Harlem to Castle hill,
Purple uniques, we were a thrill.

Handball, rollerblading,
and taking strolls around the block
We giggled our way until 8 O'clock

We dance and played in the rain,
Took the subway, sometimes hopped the train.
We ate good greasy food, and stuffed our face.

We were wildflowers plucked
from the concrete jungle.

From Coney Island to Orchard beach,
Our family trips were never missed.

We admired our skyscrapers, and busy streets.
Beautifully lit views of the city's spirit.
Shopped at Southern Blvd, Third Ave,
and Fordham Rd.

We were mischievous, not devious,
The smell of young latin wildflowers,
Blooming the city.

We were wildflowers plucked
from the concrete jungle.

From the Brooklyn Bridge to Staten Island,
We were unstoppable, even when the
blizzards trapped us.

We were young and free,
We made memories in the streets of NYC.

Seasons withered, and we branch out.
We had to up root, our petals fell many
times
Then we can count.

Corners of this city has the traces of our
faces.

Wildflowers plucked from the concrete
jungle.

Ingram Content Group UK Ltd.
Milton Keynes UK
UKHW022006030423
419563UK00013B/2001

9 789357 615372